SIGNATURE

SIGNATURE

Sasha™

WEDDINGS AND CELEBRATIONS

TO *Inspire*

SASHA V. SOUZA

BEAUFORT BOOKS

Library of Congress Cataloging-in-Publication Data on File

ISBN: 978-0-82530-747-8

For inquiries about volume orders, please contact:

Beaufort Books
27 West 20th Street, Suite 1102
New York, NY 10011
sales@beaufortbooks.com

Published in the United States by Beaufort Books
www.beaufortbooks.com

Distributed by Midpoint Trade Books
www.midpointtrade.com

Printed in the United States of America

Interior design by Pauline Neuwirth, Neuwirth & Associates, Inc.
Cover design by Pauline Neuwirth, Neuwirth & Associates, Inc.

Contents

Themed Events

Pretty Party Palettes

30 COLOR PALETTES TO INSPIRE YOUR EVENT

Welcome to DYO

Anatomy of an Event 194

Acknowledgments

I am so appreciative for my family—both my family at home and my family at work. It feels strange to call them "vendors," because our relationship transcends the workplace and the event space. To me, these talented people are all part of my family. They have all taught me things about my craft and about myself and have given so freely their time and wisdom. The honest truth is that this book or my business would not be the same without every single one of them—I am fortunate and blessed beyond all of my wildest dreams.

I continue to be supported and uplifted by a core group of these family members, without whom this book and my business would not be the same:

I have to start with Mellysa…Many people are surprised when they hear that we are only two people in our office and we do all the weddings together. We don't have a massive team of interns, temporary workers, junior or senior wedding planners—just two people. It's just Mel who helps produce the overall look and flow of all the events we do and manage the event day along with additional event day assistants. Mellysa Levy has been with me for fourteen years and I couldn't ask for a better partner.

Floral and décor are at the core of our design business and, since 1999, all our design clients use Leah Lowery for their flowers. It can be said that without a strong visionary, none of our dreams could become reality. Leah is one of those visionaries—she implements designs that other designers would never dream up. She and her team go out on a limb, sometimes literally, to fashion stellar installations using a fussy and delicate medium—flowers & plants. But her brilliance isn't limited to flowers; in fact, she also creates and builds structures and treatments including the amazing canopy for Caity & Steve's wedding (featured in this book) using more than 2,000 yards of ribbon. Leah is one-of-a-kind and I'm so glad to have had the opportunity to work with her for so long.

I've known Leslie Garson and Michael Wright for more than ten years and they are two of the hardest working publicists in the business. Their advice is thoughtful, supportive, and always right on. My two books are published, in part, because of their hard work and dedication. I'm so thankful for their guidance.

Sometimes you get people in your life that you don't deserve. These people love you unconditionally. Event photographers Damion & Julie Hamilton are those two people. They are stellar photographers but have taught me so much about living life, more than I could ever thank them for. Their event images make up a large portion of this book and I am always so excited when I get the opportunity to add them to our weddings—I know that it will look amazing and the day will be filled with joy and Julie's awesome positive outlook.

I also need to acknowledge all the clients whose events we have had the honor of designing; thank you from the bottom of my heart for choosing us. We feel so humbled you chose us to help you along the way. For the clients who are in this book, these events are about your story and about your life and love. The events would not be the same if you were not who you are. And for those clients whose events we have yet to design, we are excited to see the challenges you will bring us. The design of your event, that has not yet been visualized, will be a magical journey.

I love to learn and to guide my peers in the industry and I'm grateful to be able to continue my education in the event industry through amazing organizations such as Association of Bridal Consultants (ABC), International Special Event Society (ISES), National Association of Catering Executives (NACE), The American Rental Association (ARA), and the Wedding Industry Professional Association (WIPA). Also, there are excellent conferences where we both learn from and educate our peers. I love attending and being a part of Event Solutions and Catersource, The Special Event Show, The Rental Show, and Wedding MBA. If you are in the industry and are looking to expand your business, consider these organizations and educational opportunities as a great starting point. Either way, the best thing you can do is get involved.

Thank you to Beaufort Books and Eric Kampmann for producing this book. We love working with your team. Megan Trank was instrumental in getting it published and painstakingly editing the book and making great suggestions for content. Pauline Neuwirth has been the artist for both *Signature Sasha: Magnificent Weddings by Design* and for this book and also did a stunning job designing the cover of this book. I'm so grateful for her talent and her humor and attention to details. She makes all of the work in this book so amazing.

I am incredibly blessed with a magnificent husband and family. My children Hilary, Alex, Spencer, and Braeden bring so much light into my life. Hilary can run an event like she's taking a walk in the park and makes the event days so much fun. It's awesome to have her work with me and I look forward to having her at our events.

Alex is one of the kindest, most gentle, giving people on this earth—a truly special soul and great big brother. Spencer is a deep thinker, original, and imaginative. My youngest, Braeden is only seven and can set a dinner table like a pro and is learning to fold napkins, he's a such an incredible and mature kid for his age and such a pleasure to be around.

My husband, Joel is the love of my life—the best of the best. He jumped right into my crazy life and helped support the weddings and celebrations we design. He is always doing whatever he needs to in order to get the job done and make me look like a rock star. I couldn't ask for a more supportive and loving husband and I certainly couldn't do this job without him. He also came with two of the most wonderful girls. My daughters, Kara and Kaylee, who from the beginning were sorting linens, folding napkins, learning to properly set a table, and strike a ceremony. They are such hard workers and in their own ways contribute so much to the wedding day. I am blessed beyond measure and so incredibly humbled to be able to acknowledge so many wonderful people.

Life is about using the
whole box of crayons

—RUPAUL

Introduction

PREPARE TO BE INSPIRED

Whenever I am asked where I find my inspiration for our events, I always tell people that inspiration is all around them; it's everywhere you are. It can be as simple as a scarf or a rug in your home, or as complex as a favorite piece of art. It can be a texture in nature, it can be in the flavors of the foods you eat, it can be in the display at your favorite retailer, it can be a song you hear standing in line at the grocery store. In my last book, *Signature Sasha: Magnificent Weddings by Design*, I provided information on, and examples, of event designs, ways to create mood, inspiration boards, food design, and other ways to showcase your vision. *Signature Sasha: Weddings and Celebrations to Inspire* will be directed towards those who are seeking to easily incorporate high-end looking elements into their event, but without hiring a high-end event designer or investing more money than they want into their special celebration.

In reality, most people derive their inspiration from books, magazines, or the internet. We want you to look beyond the obvious and towards the unexpected to find inspiration in your own experiences. This will help you create the most perfect and magical experience for your event. We treat our clients' events and weddings the same way. We always want to know what they love about the world around them. Who are they? What are their favorite places and spaces on earth? What are their favorite foods? Their favorite colors? These questions are a guide to help us find inspiration for them and can guide you as well when planning your own events.

Something to know about me—I am an obsessive picture taker. I'm not a photographer, but more of a documentarian of the things and experiences around me. I take pictures of food, adventures, color palettes, art, and things that make me laugh. I can find beauty in so many different places. Look at real life and think about how you can use that as part of your event design. Save covers of home decor and design magazines that inspire you; often they have palettes of colors that are perfect for wedding design. Tear or collect images in magazines or via online inspiration board websites that speak to you in some way. The images need not be wedding images, in fact, they should be things that you love and are inspired by.

I curate hundreds of beautiful photos based on colors, natural elements, and unique details. I hold onto those ideas until the time is right. Instead of trying to fit the client into a design, we work with the client to create a unique design that reflects how they like to celebrate and what would impress and excite their guests. I would encourage you to do that same thing with this book. Use it as inspiration for your celebration. Pull ideas from the weddings and events showcased here and use them in your own memorable way for your special event. Everything in this book can be interpreted to meet your personal style, using the color palettes provided that work best for your event, and creative ideas that can be extracted in large or small scale to fit your budget and flair.

HOW DO YOU GET FROM INSPIRATION TO EVENT?

Two of the most common questions I get when speaking at conferences and meetings are, "How do you work with your client?" and "What is your process?" So, listen carefully because I'm going to tell you exactly what we do to create the spectacular events you see in magazines, on the web, and in this book and how you can do the same. It all starts with the initial phone call. We talk to the client and really LISTEN to what they are looking for. I never

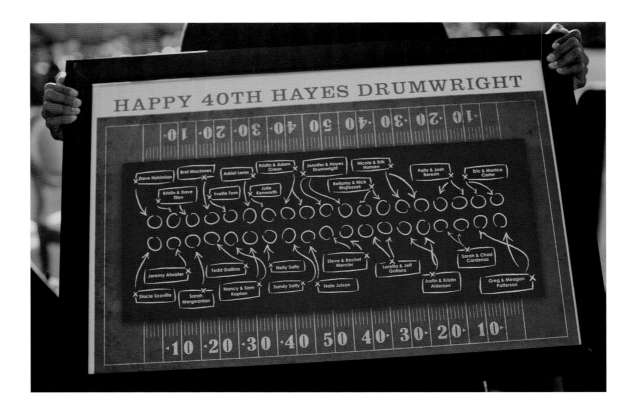

assume that I know what they are looking for. I treat them as individuals and ask a great deal of questions about themselves and their event. These are the same questions you should ask yourself. What do you love? What do you want? How would you describe yourself? What did you enjoy most about the events you are drawn to? What is the overall goal for the guest experience?

My company sends each client an eight-page design questionnaire before we start with our design process. This is essential to getting a deep look into their personality, their home life, their relationships, their likes and dislikes, and all the things that they like and don't like about events they have attended. The questionnaire contains sections on entertainment, food and beverage, flowers, decor, vendors, experiences they have had, priorities, and personal background. Once I know the couple, I can refer vendors to them with confidence. We use that questionnaire throughout the entire planning and design process and in all our meetings, sharing tidbits of it with the vendors so that they can better serve our client. We plan events where we work very closely with the client, talking to them very regularly, and we have others where they turn us loose and let us design for them. This book will help you learn about what style options might work best for your event and how to hone in on your own sense of design through some simple guided questions.

Once we have the design meeting, we provide the client with design boards filled with inspiration. This provides a glimpse into how the event will "feel," including the color palette we hope to use, lighting design, rental furniture, and tabletop design. We do full detailed schematic renderings of how the spaces will lay out, showing the client, to scale, how the event will flow from one space to another. They get sketches of details like table layout, cake or dessert stations, centerpieces and bridal bouquets, or any other special elements. While all these details may be more than you want or need for your event, you will learn the art of developing your own inspiration board for your celebration. A well laid out design board is a launching pad for the overarching design and an important guide that helps keep you focused on the way you want the event to feel. If you are hiring any creative services, such as floral, lighting or catering, the boards make it much easier for you to express your vision quickly and precisely. You don't need special software to create them and there is no right or wrong way, so experiment until the board feels complete and you are satisfied with the design direction.

The beautiful images in this book can serve as a jumping off point for you to create your own perfect event. I will show you how each of these events came to life, the key reasons why they were designed the way they were, and showcase many of the lovely details. Color will

feature heavily in this book; color is one of the things we're best known for and the palettes in here contain something for everybody. I will also show you how to "D.Y.O." (Design Your Own) exclusive details such as place settings, centerpieces, and seating plans, and share tips and tricks to create amazingly perfect looking events for photography. Regardless of the type of event you are planning, there is something for you in this book to make it perfect.

This book will also take you on a journey through several types of events. You will see everything from bridal luncheons to a Bat Mitzvah, from birthday parties to wedding celebrations. All very different events, yet all approached in the same way. While the design is beautiful and inspiring, you also need to focus on the experience from the guests' point of view. Everything you do should circle around making your guest experience amazing from beginning to end. Will your guests leave wanting more? Will they be well fed? Will they be entertained? Will they be warm enough? Will they be shaded? You will learn the many details that event planners think about to help you create a successful event ranging from innovative design to creating simple but often overlooked details that create comfort and guest satisfaction. What you want to hear most at the end of an event is, "that was the best (insert type of event here) I've ever been to!" That comes down to thinking about the guests first before thinking about yourself and what you want. The colors, the style of the table linens, the peony that is open to the exact number of inches, are all part of enhancing the guest experience, but it's important to remember that there are many other sometimes invisible elements that create an event that won't be forgotten.

Weddings

I LOVE WEDDINGS. The passion and the drama converge into a whirlwind of excitement, joy, and adrenaline that is over before you know it. Even years of planning and designing will culminate in a mere day of festivities. For us, that day stretches out into two or three days due to setup and teardown. The energy that goes into planning a wedding is tremendous; harness it and you could light the whole western hemisphere. And then, it is all over in the blink of an eye. I would not have it any other way.

In the weddings I design, the guest experience is paramount. The guests need to be warm enough, cool enough, well fed, supplied with drinks aplenty, and without a care in the world. It's about making it easy for them to be guests and making it easy for the bride and groom and their families to fully engage with the people that mean the most to them. Without that facile engagement, your wedding will not be hailed as "the best ever"—the highest compliment anybody can pay to a couple about their wedding.

After you have considered the experience of the guests, it is important that you begin to define your personal style so that the wedding reflects your likes and dislikes. The easiest place to start is with the color palette, which should contain a minimum of three colors. Feeling harmonious and blending together is my general guideline; do not feel you have to pick one bold color and one accent color. You can then use that color palette for the balance of the wedding design by giving the colors to your event planner, designer, or florist so that they can begin incorporating it into the tabletop, cake, lighting, flowers, and other decor. If you're designing your own, try to lay out a full table design before you get too far into the overall

look, just to make sure you love how it looks together. Call the local rental company where you are getting your chairs, linens, and tabletop to schedule a preview meeting, where you either alone, or you and your floral designer, can come in to create a mockup table setting using the items you have preselected from inventory. Get one or two opinions of those closest to you that you trust instead of asking your entire bridal party or even internet message boards for their opinions—that just adds to the confusion.

Once you have agreed on the overall design, it is best to turn it over to somebody who can properly implement it for you on the day of your wedding. Whether that is a hired event designer, floral designer, or trusted group of friends, just make sure to provide them all the tools they need to create a successful look that you have designed for your wedding.

Lastly, remember that this journey of designing your wedding is going to be an adventure, full of new information, new ideas, and an enormous amount of fun. It should not feel stressful or demanding; it should be uplifting and exciting. Use your unique personalities to make it the best wedding that your guests, and you, have ever been to.

CAITY + STEVE

The Challenges:

- Work in a venue where the reception and cocktail spaces are within public view and the walkways around the event are a thoroughfare to get to restaurants and shopping

- Hide the reception dinner from view of the cocktail party

- Create a structure out of 2,000 yards of ribbon

- Take a large area and make it feel more intimate and cozy for their smaller guest count

AN EVENT DESIGNER just knows they are going to love a client when they read a sentence like Caity's in the design questionnaire: "You guys make some incredibly interesting table settings. That's been my favorite and that's probably what I care most about. It's all I ever remember from weddings, because it's what you're sitting down staring at the longest."

These were beautiful words. Caity went on to describe the event she wanted in detail—a modern vintage, cozy, romantic affair, with a hint of luxury. By the end, however, Caity and Steve's wedding had taken on a more eclectic vibe, featuring Star Wars paraphernalia, vintage furniture, a brooch bouquet, six different charger plates, thirty-five different linen/chair combinations, sixteen different wine glass combinations, twenty-four different flatware combinations, plus a "love" sign and 2,000 yards of ribbon.

When we started the design, we worked backwards and began with the reception. Knowing we had an intimate group and a large space, we needed a way to make the space appear smaller. We achieved that by renting large hedges to

set around the dining area to create an enclosure, as well as setting up a main dinner tent with 2,000 yards of ribbon streaming overhead. The tent was accented with Edison lighting over the head table and four flower chandeliers that hung low overhead. Once we had the overall vision, we moved on to designing the linens and other rentals for the event. Caity and Steve

were always onboard with our ideas—as long as they had not been done before. They wanted their wedding to be one-of-a-kind. Ribbons ended up being the common thread we used throughout the event, decorating everything from the boutonnière to the escort card table to the reception tent.

Regardless of where we were designing, we always included a pop of color alongside the more neutral and hushed tones. At the church, we decorated the inside and outside with ribbons and paper flowers that hung from stands flanking the aisle. We also created a technique of braiding them. The colors we used there were peach, taupe, and hints of bright turquoise. Everyone's eyes were immediately drawn to the aisle and to the bride as she walked down it.

The venue for the cocktail party was decorated with vintage furniture in tones of sky blue, sage, and old gold. The flowers we used throughout the cocktail party, reception, and after party were in tones of lavender, peach, and blush and were accented with bright fuchsia. The escort card table was an old vanity that was repurposed and filled with wheat grass, orchids, bouquets, and braided and knotted ribbons. We were able to satisfy Caity's love of vintage decor at this venue.

Two surprises capped Caity and Steve's wedding. The dinner tent was a 40' by 90' open-air tent structure that was completely mossed on the skeleton and is one of my favorite event feats ever. In fact, guests at the resort and marketplace where we hosted the event were coming by in the day prior and taking

photos of it, not wedding guests, but the hotel guests that had heard about the structure. We had so many with questions about it: "Who is getting married?" "This is a celebrity wedding, right?" "Can I come in and look around?" and "How did you do that?" We needed to post somebody at the entrances to keep people out so we could actually finish the look of the inside of the tent.

Our finale area was a century old barrel room where the guests could dance and enjoy an amazing dessert buffet, complete with pies, cheesecakes, chocolate cups, thumbprint cookies, tarts, and two cakes. The groom's cake incorporated his love of *Star Wars*: we procured a Death Star cake decorated with light sabers and "May the Force be With You." This area was the most vibrant, with bright lighting in blue, orange, purple, and fuchsia all sur-

rounding a custom made 4-foot-high vintage LOVE sign. We also brought in a photo booth and hand rolled cigars, as requested by Caity and Steve.

One thing that guests found very fun and unique was that Caity and Steve actively incorporated their bold personalities into the whole event. This motivated guests to participate in the celebration. Caity and Steve had a truly original wedding unlike any their guests had ever been to before or would go to again.

ERICA + BRANDON

The Challenges:

- Create a space that felt like an indoor ballroom with an epic view of Napa Valley on a construction site

- Level the ground of the ceremony site to accommodate the guest chairs.

- Utilize a one hundred-year-old historic barn as a feature point of the evening.

- Create surprise elements at the ceremony and reception

- Incorporate racing in a non-cheesy way

THE STORY OF the podium girl and the racecar driver was a quintessential fairytale come true. Brandon was from California and loved to race his fast cars. Erica was a small town girl from Wisconsin, attending school in Florida. Erica had not planned to be the podium girl that day; she just happened to be visiting her family for a few days during the race and was asked by a friend to stand in. After the race, Brandon made a point of talking to Erica; he felt he needed to meet her. They spent the next several days together and then Brandon asked

Erica to take a road trip with him—to Pennsylvania to test-drive a new car. Erica went along for the ride. While Brandon may not have won the race that day, he definitely won Erica's heart; they have been together ever since.

Although Brandon was in the spotlight, their wedding was a private affair at his family home and newly purchased winery in Napa Valley. We worked with a palette of French blue, sea-spray, ocean, evergreen, snow, charcoal, and copper. Erica and Brandon wanted the event to feel comfortable and not crowded, with enough space for guests to stretch out and relax. They wanted the food to be of high quality and also offer unique flavor combinations in unexpected ways—such

as creating chicken and waffles, a favorite of Erica's, as a bite size hors d'oeuvre. The ceremony was held at the family's private estate, while the cocktail party, dinner and dancing reception took place fifteen miles north at the family's winery on Silverado trail, just south of Calistoga.

Working on a property where there was no wedding site afforded us the opportunity to really carve out the spaces that worked best for the couple. We had carte blanche to rework and retool the lay of the land. Our goal was to time the events in order to best make use of natural light and shade. This was both a privilege and a major challenge.

The ceremony at the estate showcased a structure that was designed by Erica. She desired an English garden feel with tall cypress trees gently connected with orchid strands and

crystals. The design was simple and elegant, the white strands accenting the natural green of the Napa River bank that surrounded the site. The ceremony was simple, except for a theatrical big "bang" at the end: after Erica and Brandon said their "I do's," four large confetti cannons went off to celebrate, a nod to Brandon's racing and victory lane when confetti rains down on the race winners.

At the winery, dinner was held in a large three-sided tent that was built on ground leveled specifically for the wedding. When we first viewed it, it was hilly ground, but we were able to work with the winery architect and builders to accurately

mark off and level the area we needed. We used only the outside framing of the tent, which was then draped in fabric. We did not use the standard tent top; this allowed the afternoon breeze to come into the tent. Lighting on top of the tent lit the vineyards after dark.

There was also an amazing historic barn we were able to transform into a "man cave"— complete with old school pinball, video games, and air hockey. Lounges were scattered throughout and a DJ provided music through the evening. There was also a hidden gem—a racing simulator that was brought up from Los Angeles to provide fun for all the guests,

though the racecar drivers seemed to enjoy it the most. In the end, we were successfully able to incorporate Erica and Brandon's lifestyle and love of racing into an elegant and festive evening their guests would remember.

CANDICE + CHIP

The Challenges:

- Keep the guests attention and keep them occupied with games and activities during the afternoon

- Complete all the setup for the events in the early hours of the morning so all would be ready by 9 a.m. for the 11 a.m. ceremony

- Create a ceremony that did not detract from the beauty of the surroundings

CANDICE AND CHIP had one of the most amazing love stories I had ever encountered. They met twenty-three years before their engagement at a summer camp—Candice was twelve and Chip was thirteen. They were each other's first kiss. When the summer ended, they each went their separate ways. They did not reconnect until years later, when Chip found Candice on Facebook and their courtship was renewed. A few short months later, they decided not to waste any more time and were engaged. Candice and Chip wanted a wedding that was en-

chanting and inspiring yet laid back, one that gave a sense of community, and had a farm or country chic vibe. They wanted their guests to feel relaxed and carefree for the time they were with them. And what we gave them was a weekend getaway like no other they had ever been to, in a tiny enclave of a town in central Sonoma County.

Candice and Chip had a favorite meal—and that was brunch. They loved to invite tons of friends over on Sunday and enjoy a leisurely and protracted late morning/early afternoon. The couple also loved to play games and wanted to have a festival type feel to their wedding. We chose a property that included many cabins throughout the grounds, so guests were

able to stay on site. The ceremony took place in the late morning, in a grove of redwood trees. We used tones of pumpkin, sky blue, raspberry, cream, and mint. The ceremony structure was a simply scalloped arbor that drew focus onto the couple but did not detract from the amazing natural cathedral they were in. Long strands of ribbons with handmade paper florets and hanging flowers with crystal strands set off the look of the space. In keeping with the non-conventional style of the wedding, Candice wore a short skirt for the wedding day and carried a bouquet that contained several blue glass elements.

Following the ceremony, we hosted a brunch in an apple orchard with all of Candice and Chip's favorite brunch foods, all organic and sourced locally. The tables were abundant with homemade jams, honey, scones, and muffins, along with bowls of fruit with clotted cream and

mint. Food stations served locally cured sausages and bacon, crab legs, oysters, and prawns. There was a bountiful frittata station with wild mushroom and three pepper varieties. A granola station with bowls of granola and a variety of milks and toppings invited guests to make their own medleys.

The brunch table was "U" shaped to encourage conversation. We coordinated a heavy robin's egg blue linen with white

rustic cross back chairs. Flowers in tones of raspberry, apricot, flame, and cream were placed in coordinating white fluted centerpiece bowls and the menu cards were finished with the same paper flower florets we used in the ceremony, creating a harmonious thread throughout the festivities.

After brunch, the guests enjoyed a day of relaxing field games where they could sit and play card and board games like backgammon, Uno, or pinochle. They could also play a competitive round of corn hole (bean bag toss), lawn bocce, horseshoe toss, or ping-pong. Or, if they just wanted to sit and relax, there were mini-spa treatments with massages, a supply of hand rolled cigars, and custom made ice cream from a locally sourced custom creamery. In the afternoon, guests were encouraged to participate in the activities and winners were awarded tickets, ending in a round of prizes given out by the couple. The games created camaraderie and

anticipation for the evening, at which point all would come together again for dinner and a concert by the couple's favorite artist, Bob Schneider.

In my nineteen years in business, this was one of the most creative and fun weddings we had ever had the honor of planning and designing. It gave us many opportunities to utilize our creativity in coming up with memorable activities to entertain Candice and Chip's guests.

Social Events

*I*F YOU'RE NOT hosting a wedding, a corporate event, or a meeting, you're hosting a social event. They can be birthday parties, bridal showers, rehearsal dinners, or any type of get-together where people gather for fun, and they offer a new, broader range of event design possibilities.

Over the course of my career, I've designed a wide variety of social events and they allow the designer to play a totally different game. While a wedding often includes a set of required traditions such as toasts, cutting the cake, or tossing the bouquet, a social event has a flexible timeline and no design constraints. Your event's theme or look can be anything imaginable.

Social events hardly need to be large-scale to be special, and the location can be as elaborate or as simple as you choose. An intimate event has as many design possibilities as a large event, and whether you host it at a venue or in your own home, it is bound to be special.

Here are a few social event ideas you can do easily either at home or for a group:

MOVIE NIGHT UNDER THE STARS:

A white sheet, a computer, and a small projector that you can rent from your local rental company are all you need to host a movie night under the stars in your backyard. Add beanbag or blanket seating, beer cocktails, truffle popcorn, a burger bar or a grill-your-own-hotdog station complete with all the toppings, and a create-your-own-frozen custard and dessert area with an assortment of mix-ins. Hold a bonfire and invite your guests to roast marshmallows for s'mores.

HIGH SCHOOL REUNION:

Use your mascot as the inspiration and the school colors for the linens and lighting. Create a large chalkboard wall for guests to write on like they did in school lockers as kids. Ask attendees to send in pictures from back in high school and hang them from ribbons at the entry to create a photo "memory lane." These photos are guaranteed to engage guests and make them reminisce. Play the top hits from your high school years to get your guests dancing.

"BUILD YOUR CELLAR" WINE TASTING DINNER PARTY:

This party works best if you have at least ten guests. All guests bring a wine glass and two bottles of wine, one for tasting and one for a prize. Wines are bagged beforehand so you can't see the label; those that need to be kept cold can be wrapped in foil and wrapped again in plastic to keep the labels intact. Each bottle should numbered.

Provide bar snacks for guests such as baked flat bread, roasted and herbed nuts, and artisan cheeses served along with chutney, breads, and locally cured meats. Guests take turns tasting the wines in small pours. They then note the flavor characteristics of the wine and try to guess their varietal (Chardonnay, Merlot, Pinot Noir, Cabernet Sauvignon, etc.). The guest who guesses closest gets to take home the bottle of wine. You can also add a potluck aspect to this event and have guests bring a dish that would pair well with the wine.

You can incorporate any of these design ideas into your own event. Don't forget, guests always remember the food and the overall event experience. Include touches of fun in your decor and refreshments to make your event memorable.

LEAH'S CHIC BAT MITZVAH

The Challenges:

- Create an elaborate event at a family home without interrupting their day-to-day lives

- Make the event less childlike and more chic than your typical bat mitzvah

- Bring in all the necessary decor and equipment without damaging the property

TURNING THIRTEEN IS a milestone for any child. It marks the beginning of their time as a teenager, with adulthood just a few years away. However, for those of the Jewish faith, being thirteen years old holds more significance. The bar mitzvah (for boys) or bat mitzvah (for girls) is a special event that marks a Jewish child reaching this established age of religious maturity.

We hosted Leah's bat mitzvah at her family's home for one hundred and eighty five guests. Leah wanted her event to be high energy and fun while also contemporary and sophisticated. When we composed the event's color palette, we worked with a mixture of pinks and fuchsias alongside silver and stark white. Leah's family has exquisite taste when it comes to design, very cosmopolitan with a European flair. They did not envision a sit-down dinner on the back lawn at round tables with dancing and a DJ for this event. They wanted Leah's celebration to be large-scale, unique, and transformative for their well-traveled guests.

We designed a signature monogram for the event: "LEAH" rendered in the style of Philadelphia's famous "LOVE" sculpture. We used this graphic on the invitations,

the yarmulkes, the pashminas, the entryway, the lounge mirrors, and the staff t-shirts.

When the guests arrived, they were greeted by a six-foot "LEAH" sign made completely out of hot pink carnations. The furniture in this initial outdoor space had a contemporary feel—blocky silver lounges, and Asian-style white chairs paired with light blush linens. We strung ribbons from a large oak tree in the area to give the space a softer feeling. All of the hors d'oeruvres served to the guests upon arrival were parve kosher and we set up a bar that served a mix of adult and kid-friendly drinks. The kids could stand on the Step and Repeat entry to have photos taken that they could later pick up and take home with them.

As guests made their way to the back of the home, they prepared for the ceremony that would soon start. For the ceremony, we set up a simple "bimah" or elevated stage structure where the reading from the Torah would take place—it was draped with a very light blush, almost white, fabric. All the flowers in this area were single varieties of orchids, roses, hydrangea, and gladiolas in clear glass containers. We strung transparent glass spheres filled with orchid florets from the guests' chairs and also from the back of the bimah. The guests' chairs were clear chiavari chairs with vibrant pink pads—they matched the podium where Leah would perform her ceremony, and completed the area's simple and elegant look.

After the ceremony, guests moved into the dinner area and began the hora, a traditional dance set to the song "Hava Nagila," which kicked off the celebration. Guests were invited to enjoy a variety of food stations, all parve kosher, arranged around the dinner area. There was a slider and fry bar with beef, turkey, and vegetarian sliders plus sweet potato fries, wedge potatoes, and pomme frittes, and also had a more traditional smoked salmon carving station stocked with heirloom tomatoes and farm vegetables. Everyone loved the schwarma and falafel station serving baba ganouche and Mediterranean chopped salad as well as the sushi station.

Guests dined and danced before partaking in our event's late-night surprise. We arranged a dessert fantasy: a 40' serpentine table of

meringues, tarts, macaroons, cheesecake lollipops, chocolate covered strawberries, éclairs, and a miniature candy land. The huge lollipops and swirly suckers were especially popular. Kids could fill small bags with a variety of sweet treats and bring them home with them.

A DINNER PARTY FILLED WITH
SURPRISE AND DELIGHT

The Challenges:

- Create a single space into four very distinct looks without it appearing to be disjointed or separate in any way

- Continually incorporate surprising elements into the overall event throughout the duration of the evening

- Find a way to coordinate one hundred staff, including event parking, and four full days of load in and load out in a very tight area

THIS EVENT WAS full of … surprises. Our client asked us to create an evening event that was both energetic and lush, with surprising elements. The venue was a private estate and we expected one hundred and twenty-five guests.

As they arrived at the estate, the guests were greeted by a 6-foot-tall white flower peacock placed next to a bar full of refreshing summer beverages, where they could pick up a cucumber-basil lime refresher or a Pommery Pop mini champagne bottle with a straw as they sauntered up the driveway toward the cocktail party. Once in the garden, they could choose between the green house station, equipped with lemon watermelon gazpacho shooters and summer squash blossom fritters, or the market grill station, stocked with handcrafted summer ale, Nantucket fried clams, and butter-grilled Maine lobster bites.

The decor in this area was rustic farmhouse with a modern edge. We matched tall silver cocktail tables with vintage inspired cafeteria-style chairs. Centerpieces were protea

mixed with orchids, amaranth, and grasses—very neutral and green. The food stations were decorated with fresh fruit and vegetables, including boxes of lemons and tamarind pods, lettuce in crates, and popcorn kernels. The entertainer in this area was a reggae guitarist, not what you would expect in this wine-country setting. When it came time to invite the guests to the rear of the estate for dinner and dancing, a gospel choir entered singing tunes from the 50s and 60s. The guests were immediately enthralled —they followed the hosts and the choir as they moved into the backyard.

The backyard was divided into four distinct areas—with completely different aesthetics that blended seamlessly from one to the next. The focal point of the entire area where the event was taking place was a large dance floor under a 16-foot-tall truss structure. The hosts loved rock music from the 50s and 60s and the truss gave the space a rock concert feel, while allowing us to hang lighting and decor for the other areas. The

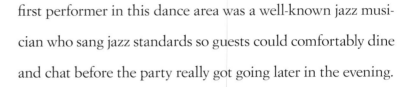

first performer in this dance area was a well-known jazz musician who sang jazz standards so guests could comfortably dine and chat before the party really got going later in the evening.

The second area, "The Trattoria," was inspired by a rustic Tuscan restaurant. This station served offerings like spaghettini, farmer's cheese tortellini, and summer harvest flatbread. We set up bare wood tables and incorporated the host's favorite flower, purple anemones, in much of the decor. We also used vintage-inspired and natural toned lounge furniture and cocktail tables made from wrought iron with coordinating chairs. The station itself was crafted from recycled barn wood and used old-fashioned electricity insulators.

The third area was "Fire & Ice," a sushi and raw bar station. The color scheme consisted of silver, ocean blue, and fire red. A chef created signature sushi fusion dishes such as kiwi blast with spicy yellowtail, wakame salad, and kiwi. There were also oysters on the half shell and barbecue oysters, and

tofu skewers. Later in the evening, this area had a projection of fire behind it, keeping with the overall theme. Even the centerpieces were part of the specific style of the event space using an ikebana inspired design with horsetail, ginger, gerber daisies, orchids, and other unexpected materials standing tall in low trays. The linens were shades of blue. The dark blue linen invoked the feel of the ocean, while the light blue linen was combined with a coral pattern.

Our fourth area, the Urban Jungle, was inspired by New York City, and featured white tables with white lacquer paint that didn't require linens, with accents of magenta in both the flowers and chair pads. For overhead lighting, we used crystal chandeliers with mirrored curtain strands, which lent an incredible vibe to the glittery space. The menu was refined and chic: deviled quail eggs and caviar, braised veal cheek with ham and truffle salad, and pave d'aubergine confit. A television at the main bar played scenes shot in New York City, adding to the way the area's upscale-New York City-based feel.

Guests danced for hours under the setting sun to the music of a fusion band, a medley of pre-recorded vocals coupled with live instruments. When they departed, they received a final

surprise. We set-up a speakeasy bar where guests could scan a QR code to get an end-of-the-night gift. The gifts were a plain brown paper bags imprinted with the lyrics from *Moondance* by Van Morrison. Inside each bag was a bottle of moonshine in one of several flavors. The bartender asked no questions and didn't engage the guest—he simply handed them their 'shine and sent them on their way.

LAURA'S BRIDAL LUNCHEON

The Challenges:

- Create a stress-free environment on the day of the wedding for the bride to enjoy her luncheon

- Design a single long table for the ladies to dine at while all feeling included in the event

- Keep the luncheon space separate from the groom so he wouldn't see the bride before the ceremony

TRADITIONALLY THE BRIDAL luncheon, or bridesmaids' luncheon, is held well in advance of the wedding. However, when bridesmaids live in various distant locales, this tradition is hardly practical. For Laura's bridal luncheon, we took advantage of the wedding bringing all of her bridesmaids together in her area and hosted it the morning of her wedding. We knew it would be a busy day for the bride and the bridesmaids, so we designed the luncheon to be a brief respite before the bustling afternoon and evening. During the luncheon,

the men were off playing croquet and having a barbecue lunch on the other side of the resort.

The bride and her mother had a feminine design concept in mind—they envisioned an elegant afternoon soiree in

honor of Laura and her bridesmaids. Laura's mom provided us with an image to use as a starting point: a flower arrangement using roses and dahlias strung with pearl beads. With this, we made our final design choices—a pink color palette with lots of pearls and rosebuds for décor.

We hosted the luncheon in a clearing encircled by a grove of redwood trees. All the guests wore fabulous hats and summery garden dresses. Our 40' long table was dressed equally well with a light pink textural rosette linen, silver chiavari chairs, silver charger plates, and coordinated pink napkins and chair pads.

The table also featured a multitude of flower arrangements consisting of dahlias, baby's breath, roses, and maiden

hair fern presented in a mixed variety of concrete, clear glass, and opaque white containers along with dried baby rose buds in vintage-inspired apothecary jars scattered along the length of the table. Each place setting included a menu card tied with a delicate lime and pink ribbon and also hand-painted escort cards.

Before they were seated, the guests sipped their choice of mint lemonade or champagne with raspberries. Once seated, guests were served a gorgeous gazpacho paired with a variety of finger sandwiches and salads. For dessert, they enjoyed petite cupcakes with hand-piped buttercream dahlias.

After dessert, the bride and bridesmaids returned to the resort to prepare themselves for the fun evening ahead.

Themed Events

THE TERM "THEME" IN the events industry can have a negative connotation. Upon hearing it, people immediately think of kids' parties with clowns or princesses, cheesy décor, weddings with traditional balloon arches and a bride acting like a princess with her crystal shoes and castle wedding cake, or a 1980s dance party where people are dressed with louvered sunglasses, fluorescent-colored dresses, and sport pink, purple, or green spiky hair. I'm here to tell you that those are not the themed events that I'm talking about. Often planners and vendors

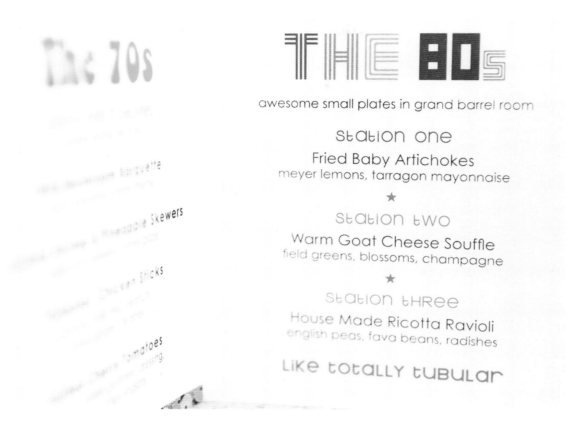

The 70s

THE 80s

awesome small plates in grand barrel room

station one
Fried Baby Artichokes
meyer lemons, tarragon mayonnaise

★

station two
Warm Goat Cheese Souffle
field greens, blossoms, champagne

★

station three
House Made Ricotta Ravioli
english peas, fava beans, radishes

like totally tubular

avoid using the term "theme" because every so often the client says, "I don't want a theme." What needs to be understood, however, is that not all theme parties are so over the top.

"Theme" is defined in the dictionary as "a unifying or dominant idea, motif, etc." In other words, a work of art. This can be a monogram, a drawing, etc. The event design starts with an idea of what the party is traditionally, for example, a cookout, BBQ, or Hoedown, and adds something unexpected or personalized to that dominant idea so it doesn't feel "themey."

When planning your event, you may hear adjectives like rustic, elegant, vintage, minimalistic, country, and garden-style. These all describe the overall theme of your event or wedding. This is all an interpretation, however. The words country and rustic might make you visualize mason jars and burlap tablecloths in a barn while meaning something completely different to someone else. However, you can easily take the idea of country and rewind it into something more to reinvent that idea. For example, your idea of country could feature rough edges, ironwork, and bonfires. You can use fabrics with light plaid prints, wood chairs made with wrought iron, or old bottles of bourbon as an escort card display. You could make a bonfire for late night lounging with fleece blankets, you can serve hors d'oeuvres in cast iron skillets, and place the table with metal chargers and tin cup goblets. The possibilities are endless.

Consider "theme events" with an open mind and remember you can create a theme out of any idea you have.

WINECENTRIC DINNER PARTY

The Challenges:

- Set up an event in a space that is highly trafficked by winery guests

- Create an event that matched the overall scale of the space without detracting from it

- Design a party that would keep the guests attention without scheduling standard events, like dancing

WHEN YOU THINK of designing an event at a medieval castle, what comes to mind? Does your mind drift to a certain style? One generally thinks of trumpeters, ladies in waiting, court jesters, and knights in shining armor. Our client, however, wanted something different. She wanted the castle to play a major role as the backdrop, but she didn't want it to dictate the way the event looked and felt. She wanted her event to be regal in many ways, but also friendly and warm.

We were also informed that the client's guests were worldly people who would want to be blown away with a unique food and wine experience. It needed to be an unforgettable, breathtakingly beautiful, dazzling, elegant, magical fairytale. They wanted it to be energetic and entertaining with lots of laughter and a consistent "wow" factor. They provided a hefty and specific list of wants and needs when it came to the overall feeling of the event and the guest experience.

When we started the design, we worked with a palette of plum, lavender, grape, grey, gold, and, rust. We designed with regal feathers, both peacock and ostrich, orchids and allium, calla lilies, and branches painted gold. We used a variety of deep purple toned linens and incorporated a modern style

gold chair with a classic gold rimmed glass and flatware as a juxtaposition between old and new. The menu was placed under the clear glass of the tabletop so that they wouldn't be cluttering the table during the meal.

We used tall centerpieces, even though it's unusual for us to do tall arrangements outside because of possibility of wind. We didn't want to have a centerpiece blow over on a table and take out the entire place setting much less injure a guest, so we filled the clear vases with colored water for weight. The water could have been clear, but we wanted them to look as if they were solid colored vases. It was a design decision that could have been very controversial—would the guests be able to see each other from across the table? Luckily, the centerpieces were slim and we had no issues with guests wanting to remove them. The pieces ended up adding to the drama of the table.

We also created a very dramatic ice bar and lounge area for the guests to get wine and beer after dinner. Guests could relax with each

other while enjoying the ambiance of the evening. Since there was nothing formal scheduled once dinner had finished, it was the perfect opportunity for socializing. Guests were offered tours of the extensive castle underground areas, including the torture chamber, the wine cellar, and the barrel room. They enjoyed seeing the workings of the winery as well as all the amazing wines offered that evening.

While this event was based around a castle, it didn't feel like the guests were being forced to endure medieval treatment. Thinking outside the idea of what an event at that location needed to be gave us room for more possibilities of what it could be.

WELCOME BARBEQUE

The Challenges:

- Keep the food organic, locally grown, and house made

- Make the atmosphere casual as if you were camping with your best friends

- Host an event on the same property as the wedding the next day with a completely different look and feel

LET'S SAY YOU have one hundred and fifty guests flying in from all over the world for your event and you want to host a get together for them but you don't want a traditional dinner . . . what do you do? It's never a bad idea to host a barbeque, complete with pies, locally sourced camp food with tons of toppings, and a fire pit for s'mores.

Candice and Chip, whose wedding was featured earlier in the book, were hosting their guests for a weekend of fun activities. They wanted something that was slightly different from their wedding, but still in tune with the overall theme of the event. Keep in mind that all of their guests were staying at the same site where all the events were taking place, so we couldn't use the same area on the site twice and we needed to be able to set up around their relaxation time.

When Candice and Chip first filled out their design questionnaire, they let me know that they loved Fiestaware®, and that the colors really spoke to them. We used those colors throughout the wedding weekend in different ways. On the first night's event, which took place on the boathouse lawn,

Candice and Chip hosted a down home barbeque with a twist, complete with its own
moon. We used tones of cranberry and sage
accented with canary and saffron. We setup
picnic tables on the lawn and surrounded
them with cooking stations. Each of the picnic
tables sported a simple table runner topped
with twisted metal flatware, a tri-fold napkin,
and stemless wine glasses. Centerpiece bowls
were filled with raspberries, gerbera daisies,

hydrangeas, roses, greens, and little pots featured succulents and spider mums with galax leaves. We also had rustic glass jars simply designed with cranberry toned zinnias.

The food stations served grass-fed local beef hamburgers, locally sourced hamburger buns, homemade sausages, and grilled Portobello mushroom caps. All the accoutrements were made on-property, including the mayonnaise, mustard, and ketchup, keeping with the idea of locally sourced and farmed products. Even the dessert was created using locally sourced fruit. We also had a pie bar which included the couples' favorite flavors.

That evening we needed lighting in the area, and since the moon has special significance to Candice, we brought in an air-star balloon to light the event so she was able to have a moon on a night when there wasn't much of one showing.

At the end of the evening guests told stories around the campfire while they got their fix of s'mores or enjoyed a quick game of ping-pong in preparation for the competition that was being held during the afternoon the following day.

The success of this event was contingent upon the guests really letting their hair down to enjoy the weekend and the events as they were. Creating these events was such a pleasure because although all the guests were on property all weekend, we were able to surprise them over and over again and the Welcome Barbeque was just the start.

40² DUAL BIRTHDAY PARTY

The Challenges:

- Work at the family home and around the family for setup and teardown for four days prior to and after the event

- Ability to provide food, music, and dancing for one hundred and fifty guests without covering up the house pool

- Deliver all items on small street without parking

- Shuttle guests to and from the property using golf carts

KIM AND ALBERT were both turning forty years old when they purchased and renovated a stunning new home for their family, so it was the perfect opportunity to plan a birthday party and a housewarming at the same time. The couple lived in a tiny enclave in Marin County, just north of San Francisco, and described themselves as casual people who like classy, yet informal, designs. They desired a social, relaxed, hip, fun event with a sense of

humor. The color palette was bright with lots of bold pattern blended together, including turquoise, avocado, tangerine, lime, and magenta with white as the pop accent color in the furniture. This gave it a modern feeling while still reminiscent back to that decade forty years ago. We decided to use both front and backyards plus the inside of the house as a pass-through, so people could see the amazing renovation they had done to the home.

We started with an idea of the 1970s for the decor and music, taking a modern approach to the early 70s San Francisco Haight-Ashbury concert posters, sparkly disco balls, and hanging macramé. We blended the decade together into a cohesive event. We also hired Super Diamond, a Neil Diamond tribute band, to play popular 70s music. Kim and Albert were fans of the band because they had played at their wedding a decade or so ago. The invitation was the first element that set the tone for the overall event. I came up with the idea of using forty-ounce beer bottles as invitations. We repackaged them in boxes and included passes to the concert and a label invitation. These would be hand-delivered to the one hundred and fifty guests, who all lived in the area.

For the food, we took inspiration from San Francisco street vendors and established different food stations. We had a Chinatown station where we served guests steamed pork belly bao buns, tonkatus sandwiches, and snow pea salad, and a Mission District taco truck, where we served albacore tuna tostadas, braised beef short rib tacos, and Mexican beer. We also had a North Beach Station, where

we served eggplant fritters, finnochi pizettas, and pan seared lemon basil scallops. Each station had matching beverages; for example, the Mission District station had Jarritos sodas and Corona beers.

Designing a fun party like this one in a client's home is not without its challenges, but it does give you the opportunity to create something memorable for them in a comfortable and familiar setting as well as enough setup and teardown time.

It's not every day you get the opportunity to plan and design a dual birthday party for a married couple. It was such a pleasure to be able to use so many fun textures and fabrics to create a vibe that transported them back to their childhoods.

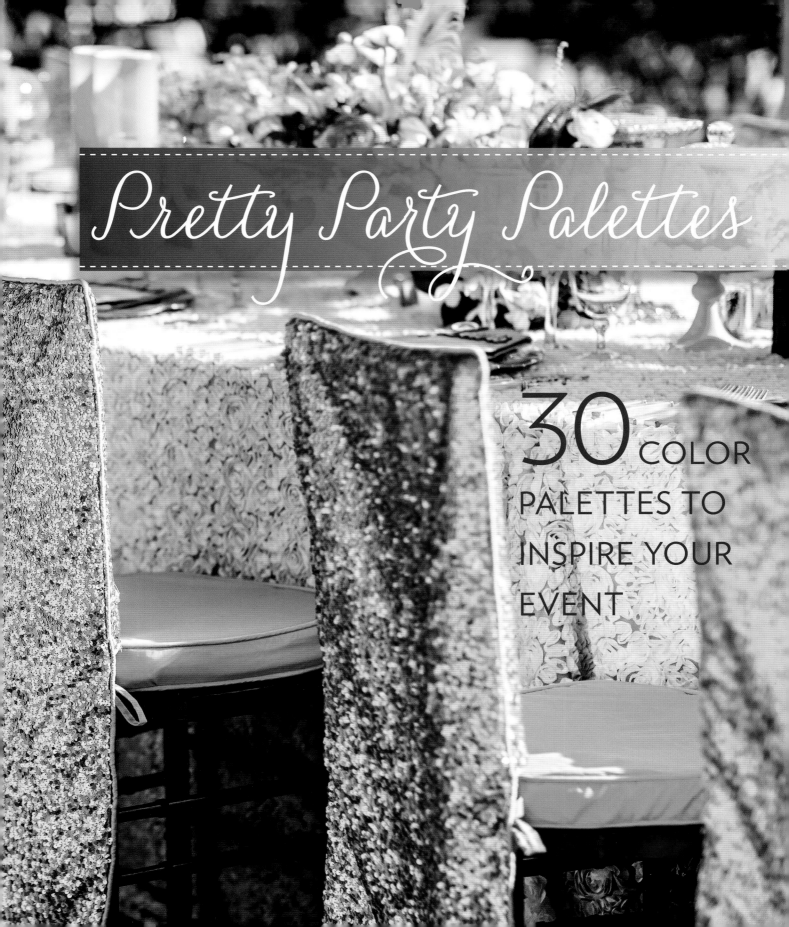

Pretty Party Palettes

30 COLOR PALETTES TO INSPIRE YOUR EVENT

IN SIGNATURE SASHA: *Magnificent Weddings by Design*, I showed you how to use color in wedding design. I also showcased what each color means, practical examples of each color, how a certain color can perfectly embody a certain person, and how these concepts were used in my events. I also helped you figure out your favorite colors while providing information on color theory and how best to describe your colors to your event designer or planner.

In this chapter, I will show you how those same colors can be turned into amazing palettes. Weddings and events are rarely truly monochromatic. Even white has hundreds of thousands of shades. Further it can be mixed with lime green or accented with peach, creating a palette. Even more colorful events tend to be a blending of three to five colors, all working harmoniously to create a stunning palette and an even more beautiful visual image for the guests and photography.

Before I start any design, I always create a color palette. Palettes are comprised of anywhere from five to eight colors and are used throughout the event. Some of our events even have separate color palettes for different parts of the event. For example, the wedding ceremony, reception, and after party might all have entirely different color palettes, or variations of a similar color palette. This creates an ombré effect, or a color palette where all the tones fade into each other, so the event starts out with lighter tones and makes its way through several shades to deep, rich, saturated colors. These palettes are my personal favorite because, while they allow us to use a wide spectrum of colors, they also make each part of the event feel connected. This is what I refer to when I speak of creating a common thread that carries through the entire event.

It is not uncommon to be unsure of where to begin when choosing a palette for your event. First, you need to find something to inspire you throughout the design process—a common thread that can flow freely throughout your event. My best advice is to find a photo that moves you. A single photo may contain several hundred palettes, depending on the shades you choose to focus on. As an example, in a photograph of a bridesmaid wearing a peach dress and carrying a bouquet, the bouquet might have three shades of pink ranging from blush to raspberry to merlot and be accented with silver leaf and mint green. That palette would look like this:

Most people start by planning a calendar of what they should do in the months prior to an event. But once you know where you're having the event and on what date, every event vendor you talk with is going to want to know the details of your event. And by details, I mean: your colors, your theme, and the overall look you're going for. Noting these down will help vendors understand the kind of event you want to have. If you're doing the entire decor yourself for your event, it will also help you be more focused when choosing your location and decorations.

Once you choose your palette, it's all about implementing your color scheme. The best and easiest places to incorporate your palette are going to be in floral design, tabletop decorations, lighting, and printed items. All those categories can be used to display color and introduce your palette to your guests. For the floral design, this can be done with the centerpieces or with bouquets by altering ribbon treatments, candles, vases, and containers. With printed items, you can incorporate your palette into the paper color, ink, envelope calligraphy wraps, card backs, envelope liners, maps, and reception cards.

The lighting is a great place to use your palette, so long as you avoid projecting unflattering tones of green and yellow onto guests' skin. Lighting on the walls, floor, and ceiling, and highlighting on the bars can be a perfect place for saturated colors. Don't be afraid to use lighting along with bold patterns, as this can make the party more interesting while carrying out your color theme. Thinking outside your comfort zone pays off in your event imagery and showcases your creativity.

I have created thirty palettes for you to use as a jumping off point. Each has an included image that I used as inspiration. I have also included color chart numbers, which are universal codes, for printing, clothing, and home goods. When given to a designer, they can be used to accurately match your color and can be converted to both RGB and HEX value when designing a coordinating website, phone app, or other online tool.

Feel free to mix and match these palettes, take colors from a few of them, and create your own. When you've created your palette, sit on it for a day or two. If you come back to it and it still makes you feel joyous and excited, you've found your color inspiration.

MODERN INDUSTRIAL

| 155 | 170 | 313 | 1935 | 293 |

This palette is perfect for a bright summer party in a bar, warehouse, or blank slate style space. Peach, royal blue, cranberry, and Caribbean Sea tones mixed with vanilla create a pop of exciting color.

SECRET GARDEN

[white]	656	557	5835	371

This palette is perfect for a more modern-traditional wedding. It incorporates natural tones of sage, ivory, celadon, cream, butter, and traditional white to create a soft and neutral toned event.

INTO THE WOODS

| 479 | 617 | 471 | 446 | 504 |

This palette evokes a forest fairy vibe with tones of fern, bark, slate, and brandy wine highlighted with a pop of sunrise.

GLAMARUSTIC

656	5245	378	260	405

The sculpted neutral color palette evokes rustic refinery. Mix modern vintage furniture with old worn wood and a pop of color. Mocha, fern, snow, and oxidized iron with a coppered plum create an industrial chic color story.

PERFECT HARMONY

| 698 | 170 | 549 | 625 | 1645 |

This new romantic color palette pops well with neutral tones of peach, cream, or blush. Using tones of melon, Caribbean blue, and coral, you create a beautiful harmony of colors.

FABU FIESTA

| 107 | 158 | 619 | 688 | 1945 |

The bright and saturated tones of a fiesta with lemon, orchid, cherry, lime, and tangerine: a perfect pairing for a fun, outdoor wedding.

SOMETHING EXTRA BLUE

[white]	656	280	631	540

Blue tones of peacock and sea glass add depth to shades of gris, sage, and true white for your ultimate something blue.

DRAMATIC ROUGE

| 656 | 196 | 150 | 681 | 234 |

Raspberry, mauve, sunshine, dahlia, and vanilla feel spring-like in their harmony. A perfect balance of sweet and glamorous.

VIVACIOUS VINEYARD

| 160 | 377 | 730 | 464 (2x) | 2623 |

Rustic with a dash of sass created by using tones of walnut, copper, aubergine, and ginger pêche, accented with a pop of lime.

PEARLIZED OPULENCE

| 677 | 1355 | 551 | 4665 | 534 |

Tones of rattan, papaya, blush, French blue, and dark cobalt blend harmoniously with an unexpected hint of golden glitter to glamorize the tabletop.

| 453 | 5783 | 4715 | 471 | 1685 |

Gothic olive, antique moss, putty, muted coral, and bronze are neutral in tone so this palette evokes an old worldly feel.

REFRESHING LEMON LIME

| 458 | 611 | 383 | 810 (2x) | 356 |

Harvest straw, chiffon, rosemary, mint, and green tea blend seamlessly into a happy and joyous lemon lime color palette.

FANTASTICALLY FAR OUT

| 311 | 151 | 813 | 2613 | 433 (2x) |

Updated 1970's colors find new life when tamed using deep onyx. Tones of electric cyan, soleil, pink flambé, and heliotrope create a fun party pairing.

SOFTLY MINGLED PASTELS

| 615 | 149 | 522 | 125 | 575 |

Mustard, peony, leaf, apricot, and eggshell show off an updated spring color palette perfect for those who love pastels.

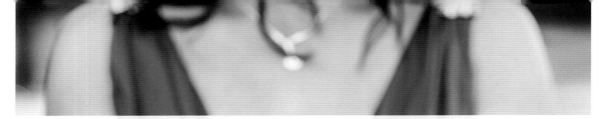

BRIGHTLY BOLD

393	1375	806	2735	541

Yellow buff, mango, carmine, grappa, and Bermuda blue are blended together into a bold and vivid color palette for the happiest of events.

HARVEST LUXE

| 710 | 1595 | 801 (2x) | 485 (2x) | 1810 |

Having a fall wedding doesn't mean only using neutral tones. Mix carnelian, vermillion, coral, and sunglow accented with an unexpected Caribbean blue for a new luxe fall color palette.

COUNTRY CHIC

1205	415	5753	411	1375

Deep mustards combined with natural greens, cream, walnut, and pine green are beautifully matched to an outdoor country style wedding with a hint of chic.

VINGLAM

| 5835 | 146 | 479 | 667 | 701 |

This palette is perfect for a glamorous wedding with a hint of vintage style—worn gold, deep cream, copper, orchid, and rose are combined for an updated vinglam style.

SUMMER GARDEN

| 317 | 251 | 116 (3x) | 5767 | 251 |

Perfect for a summer garden wedding, this palette contains mint, plum, orchid, mustard, and leafy green all blended together seamlessly against a natural or neutral background.

BLUE BEAUTY

631	2935	397	812 (2x)	370

Shimmery placid blue capped off with matte gold, Bermuda grass, fucshia rose, blue aster, and mulberry are perfect to bring a beautiful, happy-go-lucky party feel.

BLUSHING BLOSSOMS

| 4975 | 5145 | 416 | 522 | 140 |

A light and airy ceremony chuppah sets the stage for a whimsical springtime ceremony featuring tones of pink, roseate coral, and cream.

IDYLLIC ORCHID

5135	374	163	722	558

Add a splash of orchid to a rustic background such as a barn and accent it with single flower types in monochromatic tones to offset the rustic nature of the venue.

| 465 | 1945 | 131 | 276 | 5815 |

A mix of brightly colored blooms along with silk runner pair beautifully with matte gold table top and chairs to create a celebratory feel. A pop of bittersweet alongside rouge, heliotrope, indigo, and royal purple bring life to the event.

TRIP THE LIGHT FANTASTIC

| 2736 | 433(2x) | 227 | 1945 | 723 |

Bring on the celebration with brightly colored lighting for dancing or an after party. Tones of celestial blue, fuchsia, and twilight create a party atmosphere.

ROMANTIC ROSEATE

| 209 | 5185 | 537 | 4975 | 155 |

To make your lighter colors appear much brighter, consider adding darker tones to illuminate the lighter colors. Tones of burgundy, plum, and passionfruit make the blushes and creams brighter.

ALLURING APRICOT

| 191 | 722 | 4695 | 730 | 5763 |

Lighter tones of peach, apricot, and cantaloupe add brightness without overpowering color. Mixing with tones of eucalyptus, silvery leaves, and candles softens and creates a more garden style feeling.

ENTICING INDIGO

| 654 | 5125 | 5155 | 705 | 419 |

Selecting a palette of tones for the bridal party and other ladies in the wedding party creates a feeling of harmony without everybody being overly matchy. Tones of indigo blue reflect beautifully off orchid, blush, raven and lilac.

SPLENDID SHERBET

| 703 | 607 | 5497 | 5815 | 183 |

Refreshing and crisp, sherbet tones of lime, orange peach, and raspberry infuse a sense of a romantic spring garden.

LUMINOUS CITRUS

| 1805 | 157 | 123 | 1797 | 5815 |

Against dark backgrounds, tones of citrus including meyer lemon, tangerine, key lime, and rainier cherry pop brightly and create a fun contrast.

ENCHANTING LUNA

453	285	5483	497	[white]

Light turquoise, dark walnut wood, and ocean blue are a perfect backdrop for a contrast of white flowers. Choosing a colorful backdrop actually makes the white standout instead of blending into the background.

We have all heard the term DIY—there's even a 24 hours a day, 7 days a week, TV network dedicated to all things "Do It Yourself." I'm here to introduce you to a new term: DYO or "Design Your Own." With DYO, you can design your event using my guide to assist you in creating all the elements for your celebration. It is then up to you to decide if you want to do the work yourself or hand it off to someone who can implement it for you. In this chapter, I will show you how it's done from a designer's perspective, including all the minute details of an event ranging from the centerpieces, place settings, and the small touches that make a wedding day so special.

These "Design Your Own" vignettes are small looks at whole weddings and events. They are the crème de la crème and, with a bit of skill and imagination, they are easy to reproduce for your own wedding or party without costing you a bundle. What I'm giving you are the tools to get inside a designer's head so you can utilize my many years of expertise. Don't think you need to take these exactly as they are—think of them as a jumping off point to create your own using your inspiration colors, fabrics, patterns, and flowers.

When we are designing an event for a client, we have a standard set of guidelines that we always follow, and those guidelines will also help you in designing your own event. Here's a short list of tips and tricks that we use to create the most beautiful events:

- Linens should always touch the floor all the way around the table. Unless you're using a wood or metal table that is meant to be bare, all linens need to touch the floor.

- Using a linen that's too big for the table? That's ok, nicely puddle it under the base, like blousing your shirt but for a tabletop.

- A charger plate, while it is not a necessity, adds to the finished look of a tabletop design. Whenever you can, add a base or charger plate to make your setting look more refined.

- Your place settings (ie: flatware) should not be layered under your charger plate. You should be able to see the entire set of forks, knives, and spoons in your image.

- You should not seat more than eight people at a 60-inch round table. For 72-inch round tables, no more than ten guests.

- Round tables need to have at least six to eight votive candles per table plus any additional pillar candles that will fit.

- Centerpieces should be under 12 inches tall or, if suspended, 24 inches above the table in order to be out of the way of conversation at the table.

- Chairs need to be aligned, especially around a long table. Regardless of table size or shape, the chair should just "kiss" the linen, not be pushed into the table.

- If using wood or metal tables without linens, the edge of the chair's seat should line up with the edge of the table, as if there were a line created by a linen. This creates a clean look.

- Low arrangements or very heavy, tall centerpieces should be designed for outdoors in case of strong wind gusts.

- Never put a napkin in a glass. Fold it nicely: triple fold, flat fold, square fold … it doesn't really matter and it doesn't need to be fancy, but it should complete the setting.

- It's ok to mix up the table shapes and sizes at an event. We regularly mix long tables, square tables, and round tables together. It makes things more interesting.

- Long tables have multiple names—long, great, kings, feasting, and communal, all referring to a table that is 30 inches to 48 inches across and 6 feet to 8 feet long.

- There is a myth that it is impossible to have a conversation at a kings table. In fact, they are meant for conversation. The sizes are not as wide, with a maximum of 48 inches across versus a round table which is 60 inches across.

- All tables should be set for the maximum number of chairs, even if there are a few empty seats. Why? Because they look symmetrical in the photographs and to guests. You don't go into a restaurant for dinner with three people and have them take away a chair at the table set for four. They only take away the place setting. We do that too once all the photos are taken and the guests have been seated.

- Create a design board for your event, which has an outline of all the different tabletop items matched with all the linens, chair backs, chair pads, and napkins to make setup easy the day of the event.

- Devise a linen chart to go in your timeline so you know exactly where every linen will be placed. This is incredibly helpful if you are using more than two linens in a one area.

These little tips and tricks will really help you fine-tune your events and weddings, creating more successful events.

Escort Card Display

1. Use a cutting machine or order online handmade dye cut paper flowers with crystal center inserts in the colors coordinating to your event.

2. Paint or use metallic cup hooks for hanging tags. These can be found in a variety of colors/metals.

3. Use a cutting machine or have your invitation designer dye cut tags printed with the guest name and table number.

4. Tie the cards with ¼" coordinating ribbon and hang from the cup hook.

5. Place the escort card table or display in an open area close to where guests will enter for the event or the cocktail party. If you place it off to the side, they may not see it and will need to go back to get their seating.

▶ **TRADE SECRET:** Hide your "mechanics" used to hold up the door by placing flowers in front and back and candles to the side of the piece. Make sure it is wind resistant and won't blow over in a gust.

Photo Memory Lane

1. Tie or hang from tree branches, door openings, stair cases, or other vertical surfaces at your event.

2. Select ribbon that coordinates with your overall color scheme and cut to the correct length necessary to hang 4 or 5 sets of images. Print copies of photographs of you and your fiancé and friends/family both attending or unable to attend the event.

3. Intersperse with handmade paper flowers, hang crystals from the ends, or other decoration in addition to the images. Adding weight means they won't fly in the wind but will stay hanging in the breeze.

4. Double stick tape the photos to the ribbon and to each other creating a firm bond.

5. Match the orientation of photos back to back. Cut the ribbon to the correct size you will need including leaving room for tying it or attaching and a nice "tail" at the bottom.

6. Creating a focal point like this as an entry piece to a reception or in a cocktail party gives guests something to talk about and share memories.

▶ **TRADE SECRET:** Don't use original images or heirloom pictures. Have the pictures copied at a local store in case they are ruined or lost.

Funky Flower Arrangement

1. A 4" diameter clear glass vase is transformed using thread and wire, creating a unique vessel for the flowers.

2. Select three colors that coordinate with your linens, your flowers, and one coordinating color to offset the other two.

3. Start by wrapping your vase at the top where the flowers will cover. Use a bead of hot glue to hold the starter thread in place. Continue wrapping until you have covered ⅓ of the vase. Start the next piece by tucking into the color above and wrapping slightly over the last line of the previous color. Continue until finished. Tuck or glue dot the last piece of string.

4. This treatment will work on any size vase but round works better than square for this effect.

5. Flowers pictured:

    > 2 stems of calla lily gently wrapped in colored, fabric covered wire.
    > 1 stem of hydrangea, broken into smaller pieces
    > 2 small stem hypericum berry
    > 1 sprig rice flower
    > 4 roses
    > 2 pieces lamb's ear

▶ **TRADE SECRET:** Use colored oasis on the inside of the glass vase to make designing the flowers in the top much easier, avoid spills of water, and provide color behind the thread.

Wallpaper Centerpiece

A VASE DOESN'T NEED TO BE MADE OF GLASS OR METAL.
YOU CAN ADD YOUR OWN FLAIR WITH THIS EASY UPGRADE.

1. Lotus pods were painted with glossy black spray paint to create more drama in the arrangement.

2. Wallpaper comes in so many different designs, but make sure you buy self-adhesive or peel and stick wallpaper to keep from having issues with glue and moisture. You can also use printable decals instead, or use a cutting machine to create your own design.

3. To get the most even cut, you will need to use a straight edge and a sharp rotary cutter or a guillotine style paper trimmer, depending on the size of your paper.

4. Flowers pictured:

   8 mini crimson calla lily

   3 stems of fern curl

   8 white roses

   2 pieces of cream hydrangea

   5 lotus pods

▶ **TRADE SECRET:** Add little hints of crystals to points on the paper to add a bit of sparkle. Or add glue on paper flowers or metallic braids to add to the look of the container.

DYO

A Lovely Place Setting

A BEAUTIFUL PLACE SETTING HAS SYMMETRY AND YOU CAN EASILY SEE EVERYTHING ON THE TABLE.

---

1. Too often the actual styling of the table is left undone or sloppily finished. Take care in setting the table for the guests, including making sure there is enough room for all your items: flowers, charger, napkin, menu, enough forks, knives, and spoons for each course, white wine, water, and red wine glasses.

2. Forks & knives should be aligned together and on the proper sides.

3. Charger plate sits at the edge of the table.

4. Flatware should not be under the charger plate, it is separate and well spaced.

5. A pocket fold on the napkin is the perfect holder for menus outdoors where they can potentially fly away with the breeze. They hold a menu beautifully and can be oriented vertically like the one above or horizontally depending on the menu shape & size.

6. Do not include a B&B plate, it will only create clutter on the table. No bread, butter, salt or pepper, either. All those items are on request.

▶ **TRADE SECRET:** On a long table, set the glassware linearly. On a square table, we set it on a diagonal. And on a round table, we set the glassware in a cluster of three. The glassware will look more refined in the photos this way.

Rustic Bright Escort Cards

1. Plant wheat grass in wood boxes to add height to the cards.

2. Tie each with a brightly colored ribbon to coordinate with the colors used.

3. Create an edge or lip on the front for small clusters of flowers.

4. Finish the bottom with small arrangements along the front.

5. Rent or purchase bales of hay to be stacked on each other.

▶ **TRADE SECRET:** To create the stack of bails above, use one bale laid down flat topped with one lying on the side. This gives you the lip you need to place cards, additional flowers, signs, or anything else.

Modern Lounge Arrangement

1. Wrap stems in a fabric, ribbon, or bracelet wrap and place at or above the water line for added dramatic effect.

2. Place crystals, rock salt, or white sand at the bottom of the hurricane vase holding the candle, this will keep the candle upright and look beautiful.

3. Use single clusters of a single type of flower in each vase. There is minimal prepping of the flowers.

4. Create symmetry with the candles on a lounge table: 6 candles and one arrangement spaced evenly make for a very clean design.

5. Flowers pictured:

   2 dozen miniature calla lily.

▶ **TRADE SECRET:** Using colored candles for an event elevates the design, but don't use candles with scent—some guests are allergic or you could have competing scents which isn't favorable.

At Home Cocktail Party

1. Smaller tables equal smaller arrangements which saves on the cost of flowers.

2. Mixing a patterned linen and a coordinating solid color linen makes the design more inviting and interesting.

3. Highlighting a white chair creates a fresh and clean look for the design.

4. Use a coordinating color chair pad instead of white or no chair pad.

5. Use a plain glass vase and oversized glass votives, wrapped in sparkle fabric, to coordinate with the chair pads.

6. Flowers pictured:

    oasis floral foam fit to the container

    2 stems of calla lily

    4 stems of roses

    ⅓ head of hydrangea

    assorted grasses

    2 stems of astilbe

    3 tails of amaranth

▶ **TRADE SECRET:** Backyard garden parties benefit greatly from brightly colored linens and flowers. The mix of green lawn and natural surroundings makes the colors much brighter and more vibrant.

DYO

Au Naturel Arrangement

1. Using a variety of textures all in the same color tones makes the arrangement feel much more natural, as if it were just picked from the garden.

2. Selecting a clear container and filling it with water and angel vine creates the illusion of no vase at all.

3. Add textural linen for more visual appeal.

4. Flowers pictured:

   purple artichoke

   purple calla lily

   mint leaves

   scabiosa pods

   amaranth

   greenball carnation

   cymbidium orchids

   varietal grasses

▶ **TRADE SECRET:** Not all arrangements need to be filled with roses and colorful flowers. Monochromatic greens with a pop of color in an interesting vessel create design interest and are unexpected.

Non-Floral Chair Décor

1. Each chair contains:

   2 yards sky blue double satin ribbon

   1 yard pumpkin double satin ribbon

2. Chair rows work best in even numbers across, remember you will have lots of couples sitting together.

3. Also, allow about ten additional chairs because sometimes people like a little more space in between.

▶ **TRADE SECRET:** Create a unique entry at the back of the aisle by tying simple ribbon to the chairs. This technique looks great on folding chairs, chiavari chairs, or specialty chairs alike.

Scrollwork Aisle

A NATURALLY BEAUTIFUL SPACE DOESN'T MEAN IT SHOULD LACK DECOR. HIGHLIGHT AND DRAW THE EYE INTO THE CEREMONY BY FINDING CREATIVE WAYS TO DECORATE THE VENUE.

1. If you have an arbor, gazebo, arch, chuppah, or other overhead structure, use hanging flower balls instead of large arrangements. These can be transferred to the bars, chair backs, and stations for dinner and are versatile for reuse.

2. Purchase pre-strung orchid leis either online or from a local flower shop or flower market. These are pre-made and are easy to scroll down an aisle.

3. You can save money on chairs by having a standing ceremony where guests gather communally around you. Make sure to keep your ceremony under twenty minutes, including the processional and recessional, if you expect your guests to stand.

▶ **TRADE SECRET:** Highlighting the walkway of the ceremony with flowers close to the ground creates a unique design element. Hanging flowers can get lost or knocked down by guests.

A Table Set for a Feast

1. Use tables at least 40" wide to create the drama of a long feasting table. Smaller tables at 30" wide don't have enough width for charger, flowers, and glassware without feeling cluttered.

2. This table is 40' long x 48" wide seating a total of forty guests on both sides.

3. With a long table, use a table number at three points on a table this long, one at each end and one in the center. These numbers were gold to purposefully standout from all the silver on the table.

4. Long tables benefit from smaller arrangements interspersed over 8'. Each 8' of this table gets two small arrangement and one medium size arrangement.

▶ **TRADE SECRET:** Attention to detail … Straighten your chairs! Before any photos are taken of your event, make sure the chairs are nice and straight, not pushed in, and the seats should barely touch the linens.

Fragrant Herb Toss

IF YOU'RE AT A VENUE WHERE YOU CANNOT TOSS ROSE PETALS, BIRD SEED, OR RICE, ASK IF YOU CAN TOSS DRIED HERBS INSTEAD. NOT ONLY DO THEY SMELL AMAZING, THEY ARE BIODEGRADABLE.

1. Select a variety of unusual containers and/or apothecary jars to display your herbs.

2. Purchase herbs in bulk online from retailers. Some of the herbs may need to be chopped in a food processor to cut down the bulk. Think about using chamomile, lavender and mini dried roses.

3. Make sure to get scoops of different varieties or wooden spoons for the guests to get to the herbs in the containers.

4. Provide guests small paper cups for tossing after the ceremony.

▶ **TRADE SECRET:** By using clear jars, guests can see the types of herbs they are collecting. You can choose to layer them for a beautiful effect or have them as individual containers. Just make sure for an 8' table you have about 10–14 jars displayed.

Sweet Flower Girl Nest

THIS PETITE NEST IS A PERFECT ALTERNATIVE TO A FLOWER GIRL BASKET AND CAN HOLD A MIX OF HERBS, ROSE PETALS OR OTHER ITEMS FOR TOSSING.

----

1. Choose a foam ball in the size you would like for your nest.

2. Choose a branch such as angel vine and weave the nest together wrapping the branches around a foam ball which will give you a pocket for the flower petals. You can also choose a premade nest from an online source.

3. Using ¼ or larger ribbon, cut two pieces about 12–14 inches in length.

4. Tie each end of the ribbon on one "corners" on the nest, making sure the bows are secured. You can also weave ribbon through the bottom of the nest.

▶ **TRADE SECRET:** At the top of the ribbons, where the flower girl will hold the basket, place a few stitches to keep the two ribbons together. You can also choose to string beads onto the ribbons to create more of a handle.

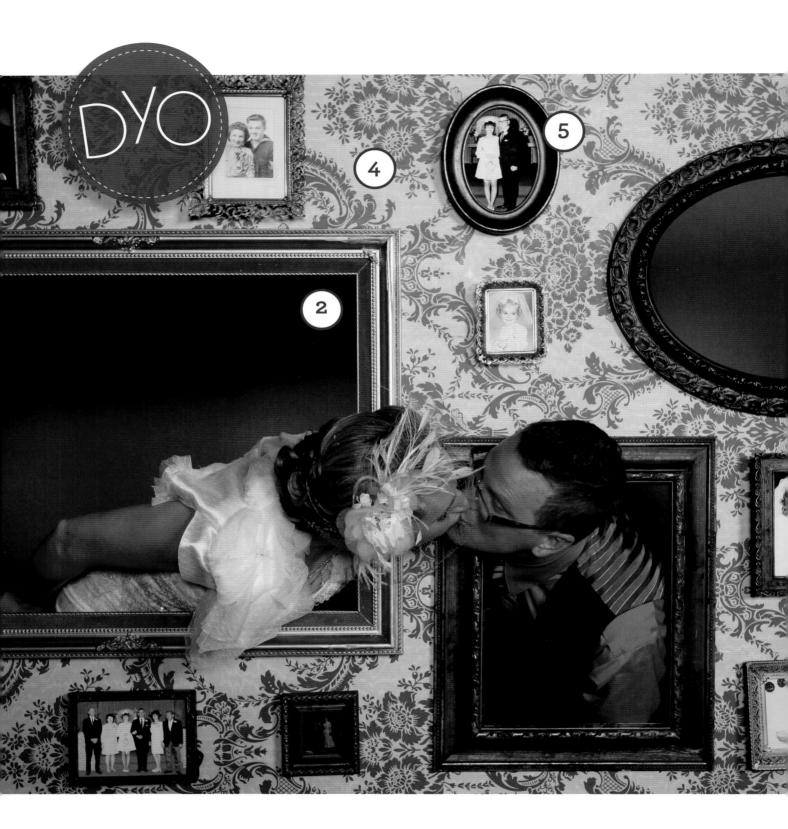

Fabulous Photo Wall

OUR MOST REPLICATED CUSTOM-BUILT PIECE FOR A WEDDING GOES TO
THIS PHOTO WALL. ORIGINALLY USED IN 2006 FOR A COUPLE, THIS PHOTO
WAS TAKEN 2 YEARS LATER AT A DIFFERENT WEDDING AND SPREAD LIKE
WILDFIRE. CHECK OUT ONLINE BOARDS FOR THE WORD "PHOTO WALL" AND
YOU'LL FIND MANY REPLICATIONS OF THIS IDEA.

1. You'll need a 4' x 8' piece of solid ¾" plywood.

2. Measure the openings for the cut outs by lying the frames, without the glass, on top
   and penciling in the rough opening.

3. Using a jigsaw to cut the opening.

4. Select a wallpaper to fit your event theme.

5. Make photo copies of old family photos and place them into the frame, making sure to
   use matte paper to avoid flash. Also, remove glass from the frames.

6. Provide stools behind for guests to stand on for the upper frame cutout.

▶ **TRADE SECRET:** This must be stabilized and it's best to have somebody who under-
stands construction to do it for you and make it safe. If you do not, it could fall over and
hurt somebody. In order to create stability, you will need to build the legs to hold up the
plywood frame with feet in front and feet in back and a cross bar. The bottom of the
frame, which is out of view, is covered in cloth. Make sure you add additional sand bags
to keep it stable in wind or if guests lean on it.

Ballroom Transformation

DO YOU HAVE A BALLROOM, WEDDING OR EVENT HALL OR SPACE YOU WANT TO TRANSFORM? THE EASIEST WAY IS BY ADDING LIGHTING AND DRAPING TO THE SPACE TO ACCENTUATE THE POSITIVE ASPECTS OF THE SPACE.

1. Select a place on the walls you wish to drape creating a delineation line from which your draping will fall to the ground. The photo above has draping at 10' high.

2. Select a palette of lighting colors, instead of just one tone of amber or gold. This will aid in making the room feel more intimate and more like a party atmosphere.

3. The chandeliers were simply wrapped in long beaded curtains which were cut to size and attached to the existing industrial style fixtures making them fit the event.

▶ **TRADE SECRET:** If you're lighting a room, the colors of the carpet, walls, or drapes that are already in the space don't matter because they will take on the colors of the light that is being projected.

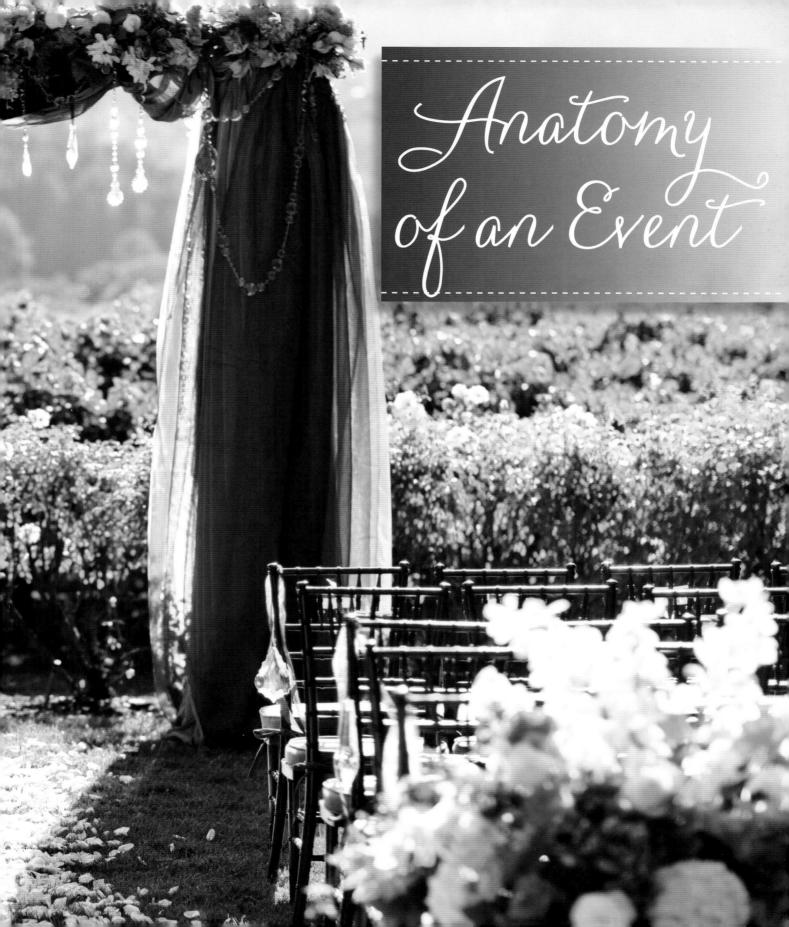

Anatomy of an Event

HOW EXACTLY DO you go from a glimmer of an idea to a cohesive event, complete with food, decor, music, color palettes, inspiration boards, and all the other details that make an experience great? This question is actually the most common inquiry that I get as an event planner. Because each planner has their own way of managing and creating their celebrations, there isn't a right way or wrong way to make an event happen. It depends on what works for you in the creative process. For me, the creative process starts with the client. Learning about the people I am creating for fuels my desire to design a unique and moving guest experience. Learning about the guests and their background gives me perspective on what they might enjoy seeing and how the event will make them feel. These are important first steps in our creative process and should be your first step in creating your special celebration as well.

The next step is developing an inspiration/mood board. This is always my first task after meeting with my client about their overall event and getting to know more about them. When creating an inspiration board, ask yourself questions such as:

- What are your desires?
- What are your priorities?
- What are your favorite things, colors, and foods?
- Who are your guests?

- What is paramount for your guests' experience?

- What is your budget?

Make sure to pull a lot of visual inspiration, including photographs of flowers, event decor, lighting, food, cakes and desserts, fabrics, color swatches, and other details. These will help you create an inspiration deck, which features individual elements that you would like to see at your event. While the concepts are sometimes obtuse, the overall visual feeling for how the event will be designed will be on your inspiration/mood board and help your florist, rental company, caterer, and planner be more efficient. Your board will make your celebration ideas cohesive by tying in important items like invitations, printed materials, lighting and tabletop, as well as unique details such as escort card displays, station decor, and lounges.

Once you have a direction for the style of your celebration, create a detailed layout to see where all the elements you have put together will fit into the space. The layout is a diagram consisting of every table, chair, bar, lounge, and all other furnishings. This layout will illustrate where every single item will be placed at your event. It will outline the tent floor plan, the catering area, how and where the tables will be set up, how many chairs will be at each table, and other design aspects.

It sounds easy enough, but in reality, there are many moving parts in an overall event design. Timing and weather are not always friendly and when we produce events, we always have back-up plans prepared for timing mishaps and events taking place outside. We also have to make sure we can create a design, install it, and strike it within the given time frame, making sure the guests stay comfortable with minimum lines for food, drinks, and restrooms. As experts in the event design business, we make sure these things happen in order to create a successful design and positive party experience for the hosts and guests. Keeping these tips in mind, you too can make your party stand out from the rest. More than just making your party pretty, you should focus on making your event functional. The overall goal is to leave your guests feeling fully satisfied at the end of the evening, saying it was the best event they have ever attended.

All these individual parts of an event anatomy create a once in a lifetime experience. Events are much like live theater without weeks of technical dress rehearsals. You have one chance to get it right, so you have to make sure everything works together seamlessly.

Jennie + Dave
HARVEST INN
INSPIRATION BOARD

REGISTRATION

COCKTAILS

**CATERING
AREA**

DANCING AREA

DINING AREA

CEREMONY

The Ceremony

Cocktails

Dinner

GUEST DINING

- Four 4' x 8' Banquet Tables
- Three 60" Round Tables with eight Gold Chiavari Chairs

Fifty-six Total Seats

DJ
- 4' Banquet

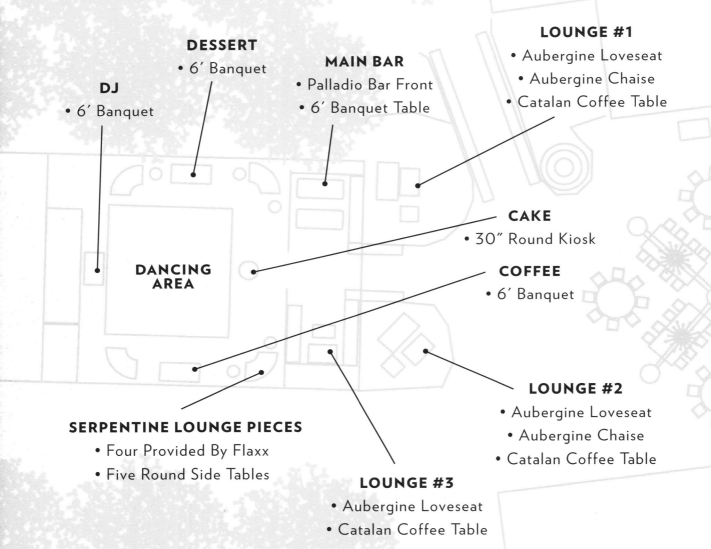

Dancing

DJ
- 6' Banquet

DESSERT
- 6' Banquet

MAIN BAR
- Palladio Bar Front
- 6' Banquet Table

LOUNGE #1
- Aubergine Loveseat
- Aubergine Chaise
- Catalan Coffee Table

DANCING AREA

CAKE
- 30" Round Kiosk

COFFEE
- 6' Banquet

SERPENTINE LOUNGE PIECES
- Four Provided By Flaxx
- Five Round Side Tables

LOUNGE #2
- Aubergine Loveseat
- Aubergine Chaise
- Catalan Coffee Table

LOUNGE #3
- Aubergine Loveseat
- Catalan Coffee Table

Photo Credits

COVER
Damion Hamilton

OPENING PAGES
Double Page Opener: Damion Hamilton

TABLE OF CONTENTS
v, vi, viii, ix: Damion Hamilton

INTRODUCTION
Double Page Opener: Damion Hamilton
xx: Caroline Winata / Milou + Olin
xxii: Damion Hamilton

WEDDINGS
Double Page Opener: Damion Hamilton
3: Damion Hamilton
Caity + Steve: Damion Hamilton
Erica + Brandon: Damion Hamilton
Candice + Chip: Shawna Yarbrough www.s7foto.com

SOCIAL EVENTS
Double Page Opener: Damion Hamilton
51: Damion Hamilton
Leah's Bat Mitzvah: Damion Hamilton
Surprise & Delight: Damion Hamilton
Laura's Bridal Luncheon: Damion Hamilton

THEMED EVENTS
Double Page Opener: Shawna Yarbrough www.s7foto.com
86: Shawna Yarbrough www.s7foto.com
87: Damion Hamilton
Winecentric Dinner Party: Damion Hamilton
Welcome Barbeque: Shawna Yarbrough www.s7foto.com
40 Squared: Damion Hamilton

PALETTES
Double Page Opener: Damion Hamilton
123, 126, 127: Damion Hamilton
128: Elizabeth Messina
29, 130: Damion Hamilton
131: Shawna Yarbrough www.s7foto.com

132, 133, 134, 135: Damion Hamilton
136: Richard Wood Photographics
137: Paul Morse
138: Damion Hamilton
139: Paul Morse
140, 141, 142, 143, 144, 145: Damion Hamilton
146: Sherman Chu
147: Allyson Magda
148: Susan Stripling
149: Damion Hamilton
150: Sherman Chu
151: Susan Stripling
152: Damion Hamilton
153: Susan Stripling
154, 155: Sherman Chu

DYO
Double Page Opener:Damion Hamilton
159, 160, 162: Damion Hamilton
165: Shawna Yarbrough www.s7foto.com
167: Damion Hamilton
169: Elizabeth Messina
170, 173, 174, 177, 178: Damion Hamilton
181: Shawna Yarbrough www.s7foto.com
182, 185: Damion Hamilton
186: Sherman Chu
189: Allyson Magda
190: Elizabeth Messina
193: Tu Photography (Sasha Gulish & Lisa Farrer)

ANATOMY OF AN EVENT
Double Page Opener: Damion Hamilton
199: Damion Hamilton (top L), Damion Hamilton (top C), Damion Hamilton (top C), Susan Stripling (top R), Luca Trovato (2nd row L), Joe Buissink (2nd row C), Damion Hamilton (2nd row C), Susan Stripling (2nd row right), Anna Kilbridge (bottom L), Luca Trovato (bottom C), Damion Hamilton (center R), Luca Trovato (bottom R)
200-211: Damion Hamilton
212: Hand sketch by Mellysa Levy

SASHA SOUZA IS a premiere, internationally recognized event designer and top innovator in the wedding industry. She is one of only a handful of wedding designers who have been named a Master Bridal Consultant, the highest designation given by the Association of Bridal Consultants. Souza is the recipient of numerous awards including the Special Events Magazine Gala Award winner for "Best Dining Table-top Design," Event Solutions magazine "Designer of the Year" and three ISES Westie Awards and was named by *Modern Bride* magazine as a "Top 25 Trend-setters" in the wedding design industry. She has accepted the honor of serving as an Event Solutions Advisory Board member for 2011-2014, has accepted a role on the board of International Special Events Society's Napa/Sonoma Chapter starting in 2014 and is a regular contributor to *Bridal Guide* magazine. Souza's first book, *Signature Sasha: Magnificent Weddings by Design*, received the Gold Award for the 2011 Independent Publisher Book Awards.